Presented to:

_____

_____

_____

Never Forget The Difference You've Made

July 2-21

figure out if dryer is gas or electric
quote for hardwood
quote for w/d
quote for laundry room
Susan Robinshel ch down
Vernon

Made in the USA
San Bernardino, CA
20 December 2019